Historical Biographies

KETANJI BROWN JACKSON

US Supreme Court Justice

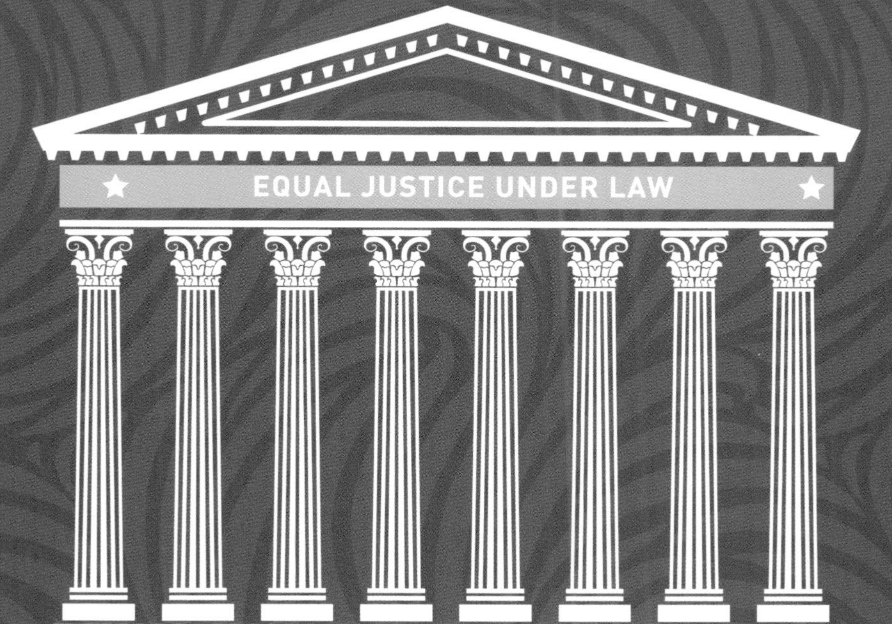

by Grace Hansen

popbooksonline.com/jackson

abdobooks.com

Published by Pop!, a division of ABDO, PO Box 398166, Minneapolis, Minnesota 55439. Copyright © 2023 by Abdo Consulting Group, Inc. International copyrights reserved in all countries. No part of this book may be reproduced in any form without written permission from the publisher. DiscoverRoo™ is a trademark and logo of Pop!.

Printed in the United States of America, North Mankato, Minnesota.

102022
012023

Cover Photo: Getty Images; Shutterstock Images
Interior Photos: Getty Images; AP Images; The White House; Library of Congress
Editor: Elizabeth Andrews
Series Designers: Laura Graphenteen; Neil Klinepier

Library of Congress Control Number: 2022941248

Publisher's Cataloging-in-Publication Data
Names: Hansen, Grace, author.
Title: Ketanji Brown Jackson: US supreme court justice / by Grace Hansen
Description: Minneapolis, Minnesota : Pop!, 2023 | Series: Historical biographies | Includes online resources and index.
Identifiers: ISBN 9781098243418 (lib. bdg.) | ISBN 9781098244118 (ebook)
Subjects: LCSH: Jackson, Ketanji Brown, 1970---Juvenile literature. | Afro-American women lawyers--Biography--Juvenile literature. | Supreme courts--Juvenile literature. | Judges--United States—Biography--Juvenile literature. | African American women judges--Biography--Juvenile literature.
Classification: DDC 347.73263 [B]--dc23

*Scanning QR codes requires a web-enabled smart device with a QR code reader app and a camera.

TABLE OF CONTENTS

LOVELY ONE

On September 14, 1970, in Washington, DC, schoolteachers Johnny and Ellery Brown welcomed a daughter. The new parents wanted to honor their African **ancestry**. They contacted a family member who was serving in the Peace Corps in West

Judge Jackson in her office in Washington, DC, in February 2022.

Africa. They asked for a list of African

girls' names. They chose Ketanji Onyika,

meaning "Lovely One."

Ketanji's parents were her role models.

After Ketanji's birth, the Browns moved to Miami, Florida. There, Johnny attended the University of Miami Law School. Ketanji and her father sat at the kitchen table each night. She colored while he studied his law books. Later, Ketanji said her father was her "first professional role model."

Ketanji attended Miami Palmetto Senior High School. She built her confidence by competing in speech and debate. The other students admired her. Year after year, Ketanji was elected class president. As a graduating senior, she was inducted into the school's hall of fame. In the 1987 yearbook, she is quoted, "I want to go into law and eventually have a judicial appointment."

SMALL STEPS TOWARD BIG GOALS

Ketanji believed that attending Harvard University would help her pursue the career she wanted. But her guidance counselor told her not to set her sights so high. Ignoring that advice, Ketanji applied to Harvard and was accepted. She graduated college *magna cum laude* in 1992.

In 1993, she returned to Harvard to attend law school. There, she became an editor for the *Harvard Law Review*. She graduated *cum laude* in 1996. The same year, she married Patrick Jackson. It was time for Ketanji Brown Jackson to take on her first legal job.

Jackson

served as a **law**

clerk and an

associate until

2003. During that

time, she clerked

for Justice

Stephen Breyer.

Jackson clerked for Judge Breyer from 1999 to 2000.

Jackson discovered how important it was

for judges to have a firm grasp on the

Constitution in order to rule fairly. Justice

Breyer would later hold another significant

place in Jackson's life story.

During her time as an associate, Jackson worked with both lawyers and judges. This provided her with experience on both sides of the courtroom.

Between 2003 and 2005, Ketanji worked as assistant counsel for the US Sentencing Commission. US Congress created the commission in 1984 to study sentences that are handed out in federal courts and develop policies for sentencing.

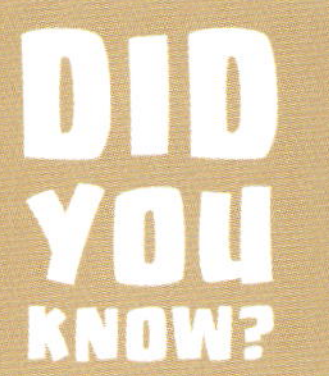

A sentence is a punishment given to someone found guilty of a crime.

CHAPTER 3

DEFENDING THE PEOPLE

In 2005, Jackson began work as a federal public defender. Public defenders are lawyers who assist people accused of crimes who cannot afford legal counsel. This was an unusual path for Jackson to take, as public defenders rarely become judges. This is in part because people

can have negative opinions about public defenders, believing they represent criminals. But in reality, public defenders protect the rights of all people charged with crimes.

Article III of the Constitution of the United States guarantees that every person accused of wrongdoing has the right to a fair trial before a competent judge and a jury of one's peers.

As a public defender, Jackson learned that many people do not understand the legal process. She educated her clients on why they were facing legal troubles. She believed this would help them do better in the future.

Being a public defender gave

Jackson insight into what people in

the criminal justice system go through.

Later, in a *Washington Post* review of her

caseload, it is stated that Jackson "won

uncommon victories" for her clients.

In 2010, Jackson returned to the US Sentencing Commission after being nominated by President Barack Obama to serve as its vice chair. It wouldn't be long before the president selected Jackson for her greatest position yet.

CHAPTER 4

JUDGE JACKSON

On September 20, 2012, Obama nominated Jackson to the US District Court for Washington, DC. But the Senate was not able to vote on it. Jackson was again nominated on March 23, 2013. This time, the Senate voted to confirm

her appointment as District Judge. After

working many years to learn all that

she could, Jackson had achieved her

lifelong goal.

Judge Jackson began work as a United States Circuit Judge in June of 2021.

In her eight years on the district court, Judge Jackson gave rulings on several important cases. Rulings in district court can go to judges on higher courts when they are **appealed**. Higher courts affirmed most of Jackson's rulings. Just eight were reversed.

In 2021, Jackson was promoted to sit on one of those higher courts: The US Court of Appeals. It is often referred

Judge Jackson talks with high school students during a reenactment of a landmark Supreme Court case.

to as the second-highest court in the land. There, she worked on many cases involving labor rights, immigration issues, and more. These cases helped prepare Jackson for the highest court in the United States of America.

CHAPTER 5

THE HIGHEST COURT IN THE LAND

In 2022, Justice Breyer was again a subject in Jackson's next career move. But Jackson would not be working for or alongside Breyer. She would be replacing him on the Supreme Court of the United States.

On February 25, President Joe Biden nominated Jackson to fill Breyer's position. Justices must be confirmed by the **Senate**. The first step is confirmation hearings. These can be stressful. Jackson's hearings took place over four days, beginning on March 21. Jackson gave an opening statement to begin. Then senators asked questions. They wanted to be sure she was qualified for the Supreme Court and that she would rule fairly.

Jackson on the first day of her confirmation hearings on Capitol Hill.

The second step was Senate Judiciary Committee hearings. The committee was made up of 22 senators from both parties. On April 4, it voted on whether Jackson's nomination should move forward. The vote was tied 11–11. That was enough to move to a full Senate vote.

April 7, 2022, was an important day. Jackson was at the White House awaiting the Senate's vote to confirm her nomination. This time she needed the majority. The Senate approved Jackson with a vote of 53 to 47!

President Joe Biden and Jackson watch as the Senate votes to confirm the nomination of the new Justice.

The next day, Jackson gave a speech on the South Lawn at the White House. She thanked her parents and daughters. She was proud of how far she had come.

Not only had Jackson achieved her greatest dream, but she would be the first Black woman to serve on the Supreme

Chief Justice John G. Roberts administers the Constitutional Oath to Judge Ketanji Brown Jackson.

Court and just the third Black person. At noon on June 30, 2022, Justice Breyer officially retired. The Honorable Ketanji Brown Jackson was sworn in.

IMPORTANT DATES

SEPTEMBER 14, 1970

Ketanji Onyika Brown is born in Washington, DC.

2003

Jackson begins working at the US Sentencing Commission.

1996

Brown graduates from Harvard Law School and begins her first legal job as a law clerk. Brown marries Patrick Jackson. The couple later welcome two daughters, Leila and Talia.

2005

Jackson takes a position as a public defender.

2013

Jackson becomes a judge for the US District Court for Washington, DC.

FEBRUARY 25, 2022

President Joe Biden nominates Jackson to become a Supreme Court Justice.

APRIL 7, 2022

The Senate votes 53 to 47 to confirm Jackson's nomination.

2021

Jackson is promoted as a judge for the US Court of Appeals.

MARCH 21-24, 2022

The **Senate** holds confirmation hearings and interviews Jackson for the Supreme Court.

TEXT-TO-SELF

What job in Jackson's long career do you think best prepared her for the Supreme Court?

TEXT-TO-TEXT

Have you read any other books about a Supreme Court Justice? How was their life and career similar to and different from Jackson's?

TEXT-TO-WORLD

How does having a Supreme Court made up of Justices from different backgrounds help the United States as a whole?

GLOSSARY

amendment — an official change made to a bill, law, or other document such as the Constitution.

ancestry — one's family background.

appeal — a request that a higher court hear a case after one has lost a case in lower court. The higher court can affirm (or agree with) the ruling, reverse the ruling, or make other decisions.

associate — a junior or senior attorney who works for a professional organization, such as a law firm.

Constitution — the landmark legal document of the United States that defines the fundamental law of the US federal government.

cum laude — a Latin phrase meaning "with praise."

law clerk — an assistant to a judge, typically a recent law-school graduate, whose function is to do legal research, help write opinions, and provide general assistance.

magna cum laude — a Latin phrase meaning "with great praise."

segregated — separated based on race.

Senate — one of the two houses of the United States Congress.

INDEX

popbooksonline.com/jackson

*Scanning QR codes requires a web-enabled smart device with a QR code reader app and a camera.